The United States Constitution

by Mari Schuh

BELLWETHER MEDIA • MINNEAPOLIS, MN

Note to Librarians, Teachers, and Parents:

Blastoff! Readers are carefully developed by literacy experts and combine standards-based content with developmentally appropriate text.

Level 1 provides the most support through repetition of high-frequency words, light text, predictable sentence patterns, and strong visual support.

Level 2 offers early readers a bit more challenge through varied simple sentences, increased text load, and less repetition of high-frequency words.

Level 3 advances early-fluent readers toward fluency through increased text and concept load, less reliance on visuals, longer sentences, and more literary language.

Level 4 builds reading stamina by providing more text per page, increased use of punctuation, greater variation in sentence patterns, and increasingly challenging vocabulary.

Level 5 encourages children to move from "learning to read" to "reading to learn" by providing even more text, varied writing styles, and less familiar topics.

Whichever book is right for your reader, Blastoff! Readers are the perfect books to build confidence and encourage a love of reading that will last a lifetime!

This edition first published in 2019 by Bellwether Media, Inc.

No part of this publication may be reproduced in whole or in part without written permission of the publisher. For information regarding permission, write to Bellwether Media, Inc., Attention: Permissions Department, 6012 Blue Circle Drive, Minnetonka, MN 55343.

Library of Congress Cataloging-in-Publication Data

LC record for The United States Constitution available at https://lccn.loc.gov/2017061637

Editor: Rebecca Sabelko   Designer: Andrea Schneider

Printed in the United States of America, North Mankato, MN.

Table of Contents

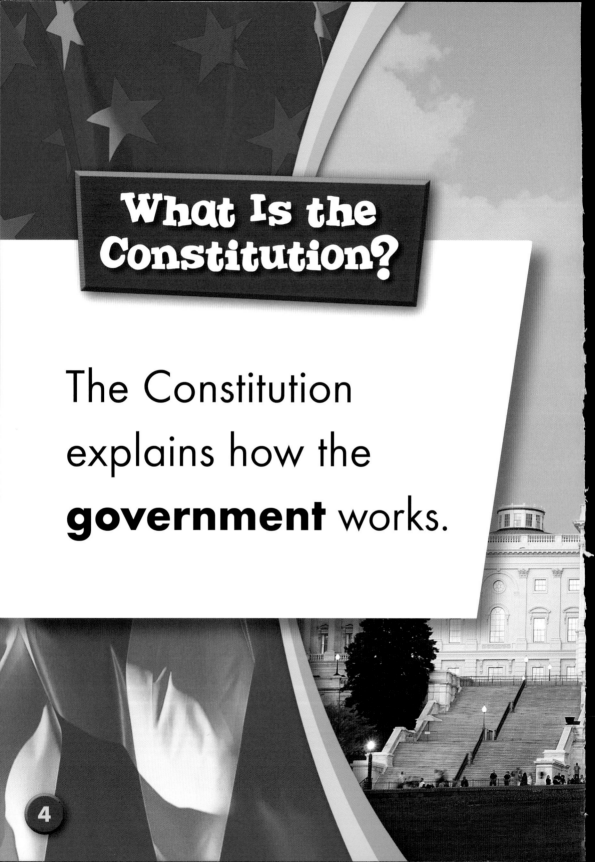

What Is the Constitution?

The Constitution explains how the **government** works.

U.S. Capitol Building

It is a **document**.
It lists the basic **laws**
for the United States.

We the People

ensure domestic Tranquility, provide for the common

and our Posterity, do ordain and establish this Con

Article I.

Section. 1. All legislative Powers herein granted shall be vested in a Congress of the United States, which shall consist of a
of Representatives.

Section. 2. The House of Representatives shall be composed of Members chosen every second Year by the People of the
in each State shall have Qualifications requisite for Electors of the most numerous Branch of the State Legislature.

No Person shall be a Representative who shall not have attained to the Age of twenty five Years, and been seven

Creating the Constitution

The **Founding Fathers** formed a government for the U.S.

Founding Fathers signing the Constitution

They wanted people
to have rights.
They wanted
freedom for all.

Patrick Henry
fighting for freedom

PROCEEDINGS OF THE Virginia Assembly

They signed the Constitution in 1787. The new government had three parts.

Three Parts of Government

- Congress (makes laws)

- President (signs and carries out laws)

- Courts (read and explain laws)

A **Bill of Rights** was added four years later. It lists the rights of the people.

Martin Luther King, Jr. fought for rights

Law of the Land

Today, people still follow the Constitution.

It **protects**
the people
of the U.S.

It is the law
of the land!

Glossary

Bill of Rights

ten parts of the Constitution that protect people's rights

government

the people who make laws and decisions for a city, state, or country

document

a piece of paper that has important information on it

laws

rules made by the government that must be followed

Founding Fathers

the leaders when the United States became a country

protects

keeps something or someone safe from harm

To Learn More

AT THE LIBRARY

Boothroyd, Jennifer. *What Are the Branches of Government?* Minneapolis, Minn.: Lerner Publications, 2016.

Boothroyd, Jennifer. *Who Are Government's Leaders?* Minneapolis, Minn.: Lerner Publications, 2016.

Singer, Allison. *What Is the President's Job?* New York, N.Y.: DK Publishing, 2017.

ON THE WEB

Learning more about the U.S. Constitution is as easy as 1, 2, 3.

1. Go to www.factsurfer.com.

2. Enter "U.S. Constitution" into the search box.

3. Click the "Surf" button and you will see a list of related web sites.

With factsurfer.com, finding more information is just a click away.

Index